D1072570

WRESTLING BIOGRAPHIES

ALEXA BLISS:
FIVE FEET OF FURY

KENNY ABDO

Fly!
An Imprint of Abdo Zoom
abdobooks.com

abdobooks.com

Published by Abdo Zoom, a division of ABDO, P.O. Box 398166, Minneapolis, Minnesota 55439. Copyright © 2020 by Abdo Consulting Group, Inc. International copyrights reserved in all countries. No part of this book may be reproduced in any form without written permission from the publisher. Fly!™ is a trademark and logo of Abdo Zoom.

Printed in the United States of America, North Mankato, Minnesota.
052019
092019

THIS BOOK CONTAINS RECYCLED MATERIALS

Photo Credits: Alamy, Getty Images, Hilliard Northwest News, iStock, Redux Pictures, Shutterstock, © Vlad p.cover, © Sesamehoneytart p8 / CC BY-SA 4.0, © Miguel Discart p10, p12 / CC BY-SA 2.0, © GabooT p15 / CC BY-SA 2.0
Production Contributors: Kenny Abdo, Jennie Forsberg, Grace Hansen
Design Contributors: Dorothy Toth, Neil Klinepier

Library of Congress Control Number: 2018963793

Publisher's Cataloging-in-Publication Data

Names: Abdo, Kenny, author.
Title: Alexa Bliss: five feet of fury / by Kenny Abdo.
Other title: Five feet of fury
Description: Minneapolis, Minnesota : Abdo Zoom, 2020 | Series: Wrestling biographies set 2 | Includes online resources and index.
Identifiers: ISBN 9781532127519 (lib. bdg.) | ISBN 9781532128493 (ebook) | ISBN 9781532128981 (Read-to-me ebook)
Subjects: LCSH: Wrestlers--United States--Biography--Juvenile literature. | World Wrestling Entertainment Studios--Juvenile literature.
Classification: DDC 796.812092 [B]--dc23

TABLE OF CONTENTS

ALEXA BLISS

The 5-foot-1 Alexa Bliss packs a lot of power and sass in her small frame. This helped her **clinch** two of the most wanted **titles** in wrestling.

The SmackDown superstar's moves along with her colorful look and attitude has made her a favorite among fans.

EARLY YEARS

Alexis Kaufman was born in Columbus, Ohio, in 1991.

Alexis had a dangerous **eating disorder** starting at age 15. She credits bodybuilding for helping her overcome it.

Alexis was always athletic. She excelled in kickboxing, softball, and track. But gymnastics and Division 1 cheerleading were what prepared her for wrestling.

ThisWeek
HILLIARD
NORTHWEST NEWS

50¢

Updated daily, www.ThisWeekNEWS.com

Before she was known as Alexa Bliss, Wicked Witch of the WWE, Alexis Kaufman was a Hilliard Davidson High School cheerleader, as seen in this 2008 photo.
ADAM CAIRNS/THE COLUMBUS DISPATCH

Not wrestling with success

Davidson grad has found her stage in WWE to speak out on anorexia

By ALLISON WARD
THE COLUMBUS DISPATCH

the Jerome Schottenstein Center in Columbus.

Despite her petite 5-foot frame

Harley Quinn-esque villain took on Becky Lynch in a high-flying, hair-pulling, flesh-to-metal cage match to successfully defend her

Then on April 10, she was traded to Raw from SmackDown as part of the WWE's "Superstar Shake-up," the event that led to

Alexa Bliss joined the World Wrestling Entertainment (WWE) in 2013. She started on the farm team **NXT**, which is short for the word "next." It refers to the next generation of WWE superstars.

In 2015, Bliss made an unexpected **heel turn** by managing the **NXT** team Blake and Murphy. She led them from **jobbers** to NXT tag team champions!

Bliss joined the SmackDown **roster** in 2016. She won the SmackDown Women's **Championship** that same year. She defeated Becky Lynch in a Tables, Ladders & Chairs (TLC) match.

Bliss lost her **title** to Naomi during the 2017 Elimination Chamber. She won the title back just nine days later after defeating Becky Lynch.

Bliss made WWE history by becoming the first two-time SmackDown Women's Champion!

LEGACY

Alexa Bliss is the first superstar to win both the Raw and SmackDown Women's **Championships** in WWE history.

TOT

DIV

You can spot Bliss many places outside of the ring. She joined the cast for E! reality series *Total Divas* in 2017. She also appears as a playable character in all WWE videogames.

GLOSSARY

championship – a game, match, or race held to find a first-place winner.

clinch – to confirm a win.

eating disorder – any of several mental conditions marked by serious changes in eating behavior.

heel turn – to change from a hero into a villain.

jobbers – wrestlers who regularly lose matches.

NXT – WWE's developmental brand. WWE uses NXT to help wrestlers learn and grow before bringing them to the main roster.

roster – a list of active wrestlers.

title – the position of being the best in that division.

ONLINE RESOURCES

Booklinks
NONFICTION NETWORK
FREE! ONLINE NONFICTION RESOURCES

To learn more about Alexa Bliss, please visit abdobooklinks.com or scan this QR code. These links are routinely monitored and updated to provide the most current information available.

INDEX